Contents

Unsolved mysteries

For centuries, people have been puzzled and fascinated by mysterious places, creatures and events. Did the lost land of Atlantis ever exist? Are UFOs tricks of the light or actually vehicles from outer space? Who is responsible for mysterious crop circle patterns – clever hoaxers or alien beings? Is there really a monster living in Loch Ness? Some of these mysteries have baffled scientists, who have spent years trying to find the answers. But just how far can science go? Can it really explain the seemingly unexplainable? Are there some mysteries which science simply cannot solve? Read on, and make your own mind up...

This book tells you about the history of the Loch Ness Monster, using eyewitness accounts and photographic and scientific evidence. It looks at famous fakes and the different theories about whether the monster actually exists and what type of creature it is.

The most famous image of the Loch Ness Monster as a large, long-necked creature with a small head. This photograph was taken in 1977. It seemed to show the monster but computer analysis later proved it to be a fake.

What is the Loch Ness Monster?

There have been thousands of rumours and reports of mysterious monsters lurking in the world's deepest lakes. The most famous of all is the Loch Ness Monster. The word 'loch' is Scottish for lake. Loch Ness, in the Scottish Highlands, is Britain's largest lake. At 290 metres deep at its greatest depth, it is so deep that it could swallow up some of the world's tallest buildings. It is more than 300 million years old, a huge, gaping crack in the Earth's surface, opened up by ancient rock movements. Today, monster-hunters can drive around the loch on modern roads but this was not always so. Until the 18th century, the loch was practically impossible to reach, except by remote, winding tracks. For millions of years, a monster could have been living in the loch, hidden away from prying eyes.

Modern reports of the Loch Ness Monster began in the 1930s when a new road made the loch easier to reach and newly developed cameras enabled ordinary people to take photographs. Many of these photos have since been proved to be fakes. So, is there a monster in Loch Ness? We have thousands of supposed eyewitness accounts, some more plausible than others. But no traces of an actual monster have ever been found. Is there anything science can do to solve the mystery?

The murky depths of Loch Ness can now be explored by water and air. But what, if anything, do they hide?

The mystery begins

Modern sightings of the Loch Ness Monster began in the 1930s when a new road made the loch easier to reach ... and to watch. But the first accounts of the monster appeared long before this.

The saint and the monster

The first written report of a monster appeared in about AD 565, in the biography of an Irish saint, St Columba, written about a century after his death by another monk, St Adamnan. In it he tells how, one day, St Columba arrived at the loch shore to board the ferry. But the ferry was nowhere to be seen so one of Columba's disciples volunteered to swim across and fetch a boat from the other side. As he dived in, a hideous monster suddenly rose to the surface and swam towards him. Everyone who saw it was 'stricken with very great terror'. But St Columba averted the danger by making the sign of the cross and ordering the monster to go away. At his words, it is said to have turned tail and disappeared.

Searching for evidence

Most scientists are doubtful about the existence of a Loch Ness Monster. Without hard scientific evidence, nothing can be proved. But the nature of the loch makes finding proof extremely difficult. The first problem is its sheer size. Loch Ness is vast, the largest body of fresh water in Britain, 36 km long by about 1.6 km wide, and with a maximum depth of 240 m. Secondly, its peaty water is very brown and murky, severely reducing visibility underwater. Yet, people keep on looking...

Water horses

Scottish folklore is full of stories of mischievous spirits, called 'kelpies', which live in lochs. These are mentioned in several old books about Loch Ness. They are said to lurk by the lakeside, disguised as horses, waiting for human victims to eat. Local children were often warned not to swim in the loch for fear of the kelpies. Could the origins of the Loch Ness Monster lie with them?

Kelpies were Scottish spirits which lived in and around lochs. They were said to attack and eat people. The monster mystery may well have begun with them.

Eyewitness accounts

Since the very first accounts, there have been 10,000 known eyewitness sightings of the monster, although only a third have been recorded. The early 1930s, after the completion of the new road along the north shore of the loch, were bumper times for sightings. Here are some of the most famous of them.

Mr and Mrs John Mackay

On 14 April 1933, the Mackays were returning home to Drumnadrochit from a trip to Inverness. It was about 3 o'clock in the afternoon. Suddenly, Mrs Mackay noticed a disturbance on the loch. As her husband pulled up, a large animal surged up from the water and swam to the far shore. The Mackays glimpsed two black humps, rising and falling in the water, then the creature sank from sight. News of their sighting reached the ears of a local journalist and the Loch Ness Monster **phenomenon** was born.

Brother Richard Horan

On 26 May 1934, Brother Richard Horan, of St Benedict's Abbey on the shore of the loch at Fort Augustus, was working in the abbey boathouse when he heard a noise in the water. He turned and saw that he was being watched by a large creature with a long, graceful neck, a white stripe down its front and a muzzle like a seal's. Other monks also reported seeing the monster.

Mr and Mrs George Spicer

Three months later, the Spicers were driving back to London after a holiday in Scotland. It was about 4 o'clock in the afternoon. About 200 metres ahead of them, they saw a long, dark shape stretched across the road. As they drew closer, they realized that it was a long, grey neck, followed by a grey body about 1.5 metres high. Mr Spicer described it as looking like 'a huge snail with a long neck'. It shot across the road with a jerky movement before disappearing into the bracken. 'It was horrible – an abomination,' he added. After this sighting, interest in Loch Ness grew worldwide. Huge prizes were offered for the monster, dead or alive.

The Spicers drew a picture of the monster they had seen. It looked like no other animal.

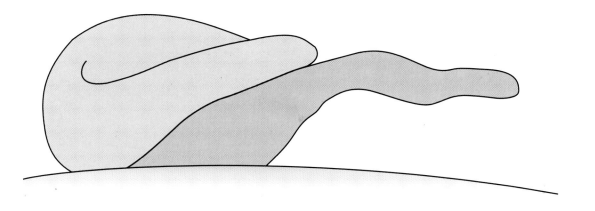

Mass hallucinations?

Despite the wealth of eyewitness accounts, scientists are still suspicious. After all, they argue, people's memories often play tricks on them and perhaps wishful thinking has a large part to play. One scientist dismissed the sightings as 'a striking example of mass **hallucination**'. But could they all be wrong?

Caught on film

Some eyewitnesses have been able to capture the monster on film. Their photographs and films are greeted with great excitement. But controversy often follows as many have turned out to be fakes. You can read more about fake photos on pages 24 and 25.

First photograph

The first photograph of 'Nessie' was taken on 12 November 1933 by a walker, Hugh Gray. He snapped the monster as it rose out of the water about 200 metres in front of him. The photo was not very clear but seemed to show the vague, greyish body of a large creature. The photograph appeared in two newspapers – the *Scottish Daily Record* and the *London Daily Sketch*. An expert **zoologist** from Glasgow University dismissed it scornfully as not being like any living creature he had ever seen.

When Hugh Gray's photograph of the Loch Ness Monster was first published in 1933, it caused a huge stir. The monster quickly became known across the world.

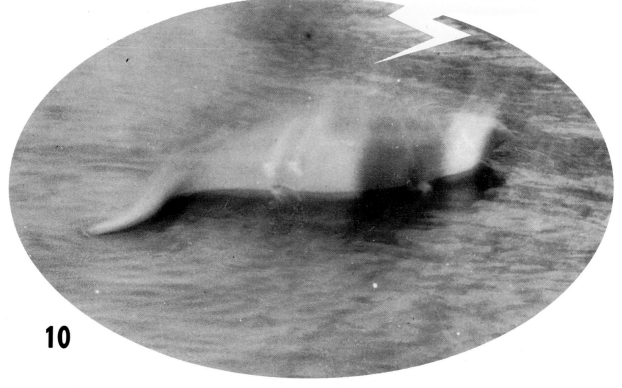

Three humps

Early on 14 July 1951, local forestry worker Lachlan Stuart was milking his cows when he spotted something racing down the loch. At first he thought it must be a speedboat. Then he noticed three large humps on its back. He rushed inside to fetch his camera and snapped the monster just 50 metres offshore. But he was only able to take one photo before his camera jammed. Many people thought that Stuart's photo was genuine, though later research showed that it probably showed a group of rocks in shallow water near the shore.

Lachlan Stuart's photograph clearly shows three rounded shapes, possibly the humps of a huge monster. Doubters claimed that they were rocks.

Moving pictures

The first moving pictures of Nessie were taken in April 1960 by engineer Tim Dinsdale. Using a 16-mm cine-camera, he took several metres of film showing a hump swimming away from him. When shown on television, it caused a huge stir. But did it really show a monster?

Six years later, the film was analysed by British Royal Air Force Intelligence which reported that the object was not a boat or submarine but 'probably **animate***'. It was about 1.7 m wide and was moving at about 16 km per hour. It was also examined by computer-enhancement experts at* **NASA** *who spotted two other parts which could belong to a body, apart from the main hump. Many people were convinced that this was the monster.*

It's official!

Interest in Loch Ness continued to grow in the 1960s and '70s with a new generation of monster-hunters. Despite the doubts of many scientists, serious expeditions were organized by universities and local biologists to scour the loch in search of proof that the monster existed, or equally, that it did not.

Since the 1930s, thousands of people have visited Loch Ness in the hope of glimpsing the monster. Their starting point is often the Loch Ness Visitor Centre on the shore of the loch.

A full-time job

In 1969, Londoner Frank Searle gave up his job to camp full-time by Loch Ness. In 1971 his patience was rewarded. He described the monster as being 'seven feet long, dark and knobbly on top, smooth dirty white underneath'. More sightings followed and a series of photographs. Sadly, the films later proved to have been tampered with. In some, an extra hump had been **superimposed** on to the original photo!

Monster bureau

In 1961, the Loch Ness Investigation Bureau was founded by British **naturalist** Sir Peter Scott, to explore the loch more systematically. The Bureau collected all the existing sightings and organized a long-term watch over the lake. Night after night, teams of scientists scoured the loch with searchlights and **sonar**. They detected several large objects in the water but could not identify what they were.

The Loch Ness Project

The Loch Ness Project was founded in 1978. It organizes field trips for students who volunteer to work on the loch. One of their tasks is to take samples of the **sediment** on the bottom of the loch. These are used for finding out more about the history of the loch which may help to determine what type of creature the monster could be. The leader of the Project is naturalist Adrian Shine. After 20 years of searching, he is now convinced that there is no Loch Ness Monster to be found.

Playing tricks

*One of the problems with eyewitness evidence is that the loch itself plays tricks on the eyes. On a calm day, the steep shorelines cause deceptive shadows and reflections. These can make objects such as water birds, otters, boat **wakes** and waves appear much bigger or longer than they actually are. Logs, mats of floating vegetation, and even motorboats have also been mistaken for monsters. So, is the monster an **optical illusion**, or a case of mistaken identity as many scientists suspect?*

A European otter.

Searching underwater

For people determined to find a monster in Loch Ness, the best place to look is, of course, under the water. If a monster does exist, this is where it must spend most of its time. Sending human divers down into the loch is a risky business. The water is very cold, very deep and very murky. Scientists have had to find other ways of exploring the loch. The two most effective methods used so far are **sonar** searching and underwater photography.

How sonar works

The word sonar stands for sound navigation and ranging. A sonar machine on board a boat sends out a pulse of sound in a narrow beam and listens for echoes as the sound bounces off objects in the water. From the time it takes for any echo to return, the machine works out how far away the objects are. The direction and distance of the objects appear on a screen. Sonar can also give an idea of an object's size, shape and speed. Some sonar machines can be towed alongside the boat to give a wider coverage.

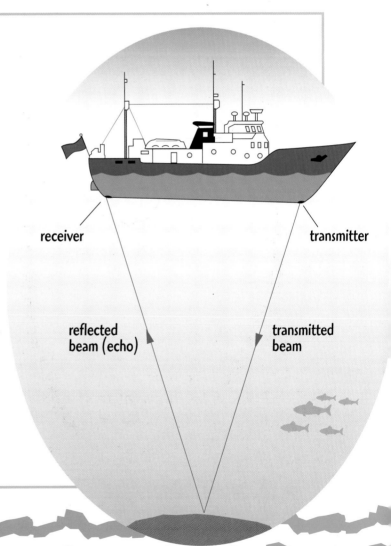

receiver

transmitter

reflected beam (echo)

transmitted beam

Sonar searching

The first scientific expedition to Loch Ness was organized in 1959 by the Natural History Museum in London. Using sonar, scientists detected a large object just under the water's surface. They tracked it as it dived to a depth of 20 metres and then rose back up again. The object may have been a shoal of fish. A more recent expedition was Operation Deepscan in 1987. A **flotilla** of 24 launches, equipped with sonar, spent a week patrolling the loch. They detected a mysterious object which they described as being 'the size of a large shark'.

A row of sonar boats, scanning Loch Ness in search of a monster, during Operation Deepscan in 1987. Various mysterious, and still unidentified, objects were detected in the water.

Mistaken identity?

Hundreds of sonar 'hits' have been made. You can even hire your own monster-hunting boat from the loch shore, complete with sonar equipment. These hits seem to show that there are large animals living in Loch Ness. But, scientifically, they still do not represent concrete proof. Most of them could easily have been made by large shoals of fish, rising bubbles of gas in the water or even giant underwater waves. Some, however, including three detected by Operation Deepscan, are yet to be identified...

Underwater photography

In 1972 and 1975, a team of scientists from the Academy of
Applied Science, based in Massachusetts, USA, and led by
Dr Robert Rines, made a series of trips to Loch Ness.
Working with the Loch Ness Investigation Bureau, they set
up automatic cameras under the water to flash
every few seconds or so, or whenever their
sonar detected objects moving nearby.
To their great excitement, several of the
photographs appeared to show parts of
a large creature.

*Robert Rines fixed an
underwater camera to a frame
on his return to Loch Ness in 1980.
Taking photographs underwater
was made more difficult by the
loch's murky water.*

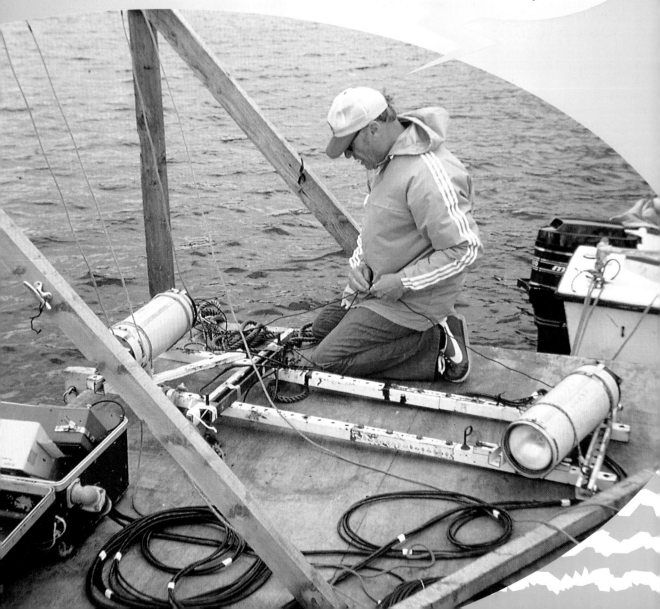

The flipper picture

*One of the 1972 photographs seemed to show a large, diamond-shaped flipper. The 1975 photos showed the head and body of a large creature, which led **naturalist** Sir Peter Scott to suggest that the monster might have been a **plesiosaur**, a prehistoric reptile thought to be long extinct (see pages 18 and 19). The photographs were sent to other leading **zoologists** and even debated in the British Parliament. One scientist went as far as to say that the photos seemed to indicate the presence of large animals in the loch but were not sufficient to identify them. Others were not so sure.*

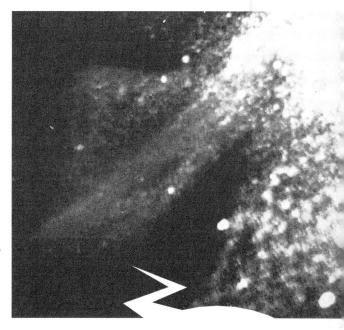

Could this be the Loch Ness Monster? Rines' famous photograph, taken in 1972, seemed to show a flipper belonging to a large, swimming creature.

Return to Loch Ness

In 1997, Robert Rines returned to Loch Ness to try to prove once and for all that something was lurking in its water. With him, he brought Charles Wyckoff, a photographic pioneer who had developed the techniques needed to photograph nuclear bomb explosions and the surface of the Moon. The aim was to sweep the loch with sonar, then relay the results to a **GPS** (Global Positioning System) on the shore to give any object's exact location. The camera crew would follow close behind. Although the sonar detected several large, moving targets which the team's **marine biologist** could not explain as shoals of fish, taking clear photographs proved a much trickier task. The murky water limited visibility to a metre or so, and moisture seeped in and ruined the cameras. So, the mystery remains to be solved.

What is it?

What type of monster do eyewitnesses claim to have seen? Their reports are remarkably similar, often describing a large, long-necked, hump-backed creature. It sometimes swims at speed, with its neck raised or lowered, and sometimes sinks down beneath the water. Could it indeed be a **plesiosaur**, as Sir Peter Scott suggested? Or does the scientific evidence rule this out?

For and against

Plesiosaurs were long-necked reptiles which lived in warm, inland seas during **prehistoric** times. They were thought to have died out some 70 million years ago, at about the same time as the dinosaurs. But there is no absolute proof that they do not still exist and their shape certainly matches the photographs and descriptions of the Loch Ness Monster.

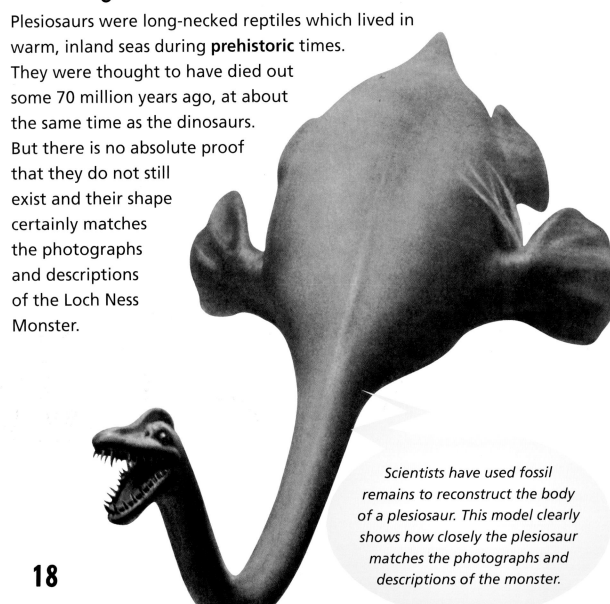

Scientists have used fossil remains to reconstruct the body of a plesiosaur. This model clearly shows how closely the plesiosaur matches the photographs and descriptions of the monster.

So, could a small group of plesiosaurs have escaped **extinction** by sheltering in Loch Ness, unknown to science? It seems unlikely. Firstly, reptiles are cold-blooded animals. They rely on the weather to warm their bodies so that they can function properly. They would find it hard to live in the freezing cold water of Loch Ness. No reptile is known that could survive such cold conditions. Secondly, the **geological** history of the loch also seems to rule them out. For much of the time since the time of the dinosaurs, Loch Ness has been filled with solid ice as a result of a succession of **Ice Ages**. However, when the ice finally retreated about 11,000 years ago, it left the loch and a shallow passage to the sea – the River Ness. Could the plesiosaurs have swum up the river from the sea and entered the loch? It seems unlikely, though not impossible.

Other 'lost' animals

Cryptozoology is the study of cryptids, or 'unknown' animals. This means animals thought to be long extinct. One example is a fish called the coelacanth. Thought to have died out 70 million years ago, a living coelacanth was caught in the Indian Ocean in 1938. Scientists were amazed. If the coelacanth still exists, what about other prehistoric animals? Could there be a plesiosaur still living in Loch Ness?

A coelacanth.

Mammals and fish

If science rules out the **plesiosaur**, what other type of creature could the monster be? Other possible candidates include mammals and fish.

A mammal?

Some scientists think that the Loch Ness Monster might be a large mammal, such as a whale. Mammals are warm-blooded so would be able to adapt to the cold conditions. But the largest whales are **filter-feeders**, feeding on **plankton** in the water. The small amount of plankton in Loch Ness means that the monster could not be one of these (see box below). Other mammals, such as seals, need to leave the water to breed, and there have been no sightings or traces of young. If the monster does exist, it must be part of a group to breed and continue the line. Mammals also need to surface frequently to breathe, so there should have been far more sightings of the creature if it is a mammal.

Finding food

*If a large creature exists in Loch Ness, it probably eats fish. But it seems unlikely that the loch's fish supply is large enough to support a large **predator**. Despite the loch's great size, the water is poor in **nutrients** to start the food chain. There is very little light for plant plankton to grow, and, therefore, little for animal plankton to feed on, which in turn provides food for larger creatures such as fish. As a result, there are very few fish for such a large lake, or for a hungry monster.*

A fish?

If there is a large creature in Loch Ness, it is more likely to be a large fish. Some people think that it could be a giant eel or a Baltic sturgeon, the largest types of fish found in fresh water. It is possible that the sturgeon enters the loch looking for a mate. When it does not find one, it swims out to sea again. Both types of fish can grow more than 3 metres long. However, none of the descriptions of sightings match any known fish closely. What scientists need is to examine a specimen or some actual remains of the creature, and nothing has been found so far.

Among the largest fish are basking sharks which, like whales, feed on plankton. They can reach more than 11 metres in length. They regularly appear in British waters in summer, when they swim inshore during their annual **migration**. In winter, they disappear again. One theory is that they move into deep water to **hibernate**. Could this deep water be Loch Ness?

The huge mouth of a basking shark, one of the biggest fish in the sea. If scientists could prove that these creatures spend the winter in Loch Ness, the monster mystery could be solved.

Waves, wakes and waterspouts

People who do not believe that the loch is home to a large, mysterious creature put down many of the eyewitness sightings to odd waves and shadows on the loch's surface, the **wakes** left by passing boats, or weird weather **phenomena**. So, just how misleading can these be?

Waves and wakes

In rough weather, the wakes from passing boats are quickly broken up by the wind and waves. But on calm days – on which most monster sightings have been reported – the wakes last longer and appear much bigger. From low down, the wake can look like a rippling row of humps travelling across the water. Could these explain the many accounts of a hump-backed monster? Large waves breaking in the shallows may also be mistaken for a swimming body.

This wake was photographed on Loch Ness in August 1996. Mysteriously, it was a clear day with no wind, and there were no boats passing nearby.

Waterspouts

Waterspouts are spinning funnels of water, sucked up by thunder clouds when they pass over water. The tallest ever seen was an amazing 1.5 kilometres high. At sea, terrified sailors often mistook them for monsters. Water devils are smaller versions of waterspouts. They spin across the water, whipping up spouts of water, up to about 3 metres high. British tornado and whirlwind expert, Dr Terence Meaden, believes that water devils may help to explain the mystery of the Loch Ness Monster. Their long, tapering, funnel shape could easily be mistaken for a monster's long, thin head and neck. Water devils also cause the surface of the water to bubble and froth. Could the rings of bubbles suggest a monster's humps?

Seeing things?

*A mirage is an image of an object which is not really there. People have seen boats, buildings, and perhaps even monsters, as a result of these **optical illusions**. Mirages are caused by changes in temperature in different layers of air, lying over land or water. Light rays coming from existing objects can be bent up or down as they pass through the layers. Your brain is tricked into thinking that the distorted reflection looks like another object. For example, you may think you see a puddle of water on the road on a hot, summer's day. What you are actually seeing is a mirage of the sky. Could 'Nessie' be the result of a mirage?*

Monster fakes

Many of the eyewitness sightings and photographs of the Loch Ness Monster have turned out to be fakes. Some are cases of mistaken identity, rather than deliberate hoaxes. But some have been carefully planned to deceive. Why do people do it? The obvious reasons are to gain fame or money. One person even went as far as to suggest that the monster was an elaborate hoax dreamt up by the Scottish Tourist Board to attract more visitors to the Highlands! Needless to say, this has been strongly denied.

The surgeon's photograph

One of the most famous photographs of the Loch Ness Monster appeared in April 1934. Nicknamed 'the surgeon's photograph', it was taken by London surgeon, Robert Kenneth Wilson. The photo clearly showed a long neck, with a tiny head, arched over the water. When the photograph was printed in the *Daily Mail*, it caused a sensation. But was it real? Many people thought so.

The most famous of all monster pictures is the so-called 'surgeon's photograph'. In 1994, the photograph was claimed to be a fake but some experts have dismissed these claims. Is it a fake or is it genuine? The controversy continues.

In 1994, Loch Ness researcher, Alisdair Boyd, claimed that the photo was an elaborate fake. His enquiries led to a man called Christian Spurling who confessed to helping the surgeon plan the hoax in order to trick the newspapers. He said that the object in the photo was, in fact, a 30-centimetre plastic neck, attached to a toy submarine, and not a monster at all. To answer his critics, Boyd set out to prove his theory. From the shape of the ripples around the neck, it was possible to calculate the angle at which the photo had been taken. Boyd lined up his camera and took some pictures of a 30-centimetre styrofoam neck he had placed in the water. The results were almost identical. Despite this, Boyd remains convinced that there is a monster in Loch Ness and claims to have seen it.

Monster footprints

In December 1933, there was great excitement at the discovery of a set of monster-sized footprints on the loch shore. They were later found to have been created using an umbrella stand made from the stuffed back foot of a hippopotamus!

What's in a name?

Based on the **rhomboid,** or diamond, shape of the flipper in Rines' famous photograph, **naturalist** Sir Peter Scott suggested a scientific Latin name for the monster – Nessiteras rhombopteryx. Doubters discovered that you could rearrange the letters to read 'Monster hoax by Sir Peter S'!

Other lake monsters

Loch Ness is not the only lake where long-necked monsters are thought to lurk. Similar creatures have been sighted not only in other Scottish lochs, but in about 300 lakes all over the world, from Europe to South-East Asia. If hard proof was found for any of these, it would give a huge boost to the search for the monster in Loch Ness.

Lake Okanagan, Canada

Lake Okanagan in western Canada is thought to contain a monster called Ogopogo. Hundreds of sightings have been recorded. In July 1986, a man fishing on the lake reported, 'It looked like a submarine surfacing, coming towards my boat. As it came up, we could see six humps out of the water, each one creating a wake'. One woman reported almost running over it as she was out water-skiing. The local Okanakane Indians have many myths about a lake serpent. When crossing the lake by canoe, legend says, travellers always took a chicken or dog to sacrifice if the monster came too close.

A lakeside model of Ogopogo, the monster in Lake Okanagan, Canada. Sightings of this monster rival those of Nessie.

Lake Champlain, USA

Stories of a monster in Lake Champlain in Vermont, USA, also go back hundreds of years. Nicknamed 'Champ', the monster is often described as having a long, sinuous neck, with a dark body and several humps. The most convincing evidence for Champ's existence was a photograph taken in 1977 which showed a huge, long-necked creature. Despite close scientific analysis, the photo shows no sign of being faked in any way. Whether you see the monster or not, you can always tuck into some 'Champ's chips' (made to a secret recipe) or listen to Champ 101.3 FM, the monster's own radio station, instead!

This photo, taken in 1977, added fuel to the rumour that there was a monster living in Lake Champlain.

Lake Ikeda, Japan

The first photograph of Issie, the monster in Lake Ikeda, on the island of Honshu, Japan, was taken by holiday-maker Mr Matsubara in 1978. Legend says that Issie was once a beautiful white horse living by the lake. One day, a Samurai warrior took her foal away. In despair, Issie jumped into the lake, occasionally surfacing, in the form of a dark, humped monster, to look for her foal.

In conclusion

So, can science really solve the mystery of the Loch Ness Monster? Despite the thousands of eyewitness accounts and photographic evidence, scientists remain unconvinced. Eyewitnesses are often unreliable and photographs are relatively easy to fake. In the absence of concrete proof, such as an actual specimen, or a skeleton, the monster seems fated to remain a myth.

But while science cannot seem to solve the mystery, for now at least, it cannot prove that a large creature of some sort does not exist in the loch. Can all the eyewitnesses be wrong? Many were respectable, reliable people, with no reason to make up their stories. Or was the loch itself playing tricks on them, turning boat **wakes**, waves and water devils into hump-backed monsters?

Those who claim to have seen the Loch Ness Monster do not have any doubts at all, whether science agrees or not. They believe that something large and alive is lurking in Loch Ness. After all, there are plenty of places for it to hide.

The search for the Loch Ness Monster continues. This is a sonar research ship used by Project Urquhart to scan the loch in 1992. Several expeditions have got tantalizingly close to finding something. But what that something is, nobody yet knows.

What do you think?

Now that you have read about the Loch Ness Monster and the possible explanations for it, can you draw any conclusions? Do you believe that a monster could exist? Do you have any theories of your own?

What about the eyewitness accounts? Do you think they were accurate or **optical illusions**? Could any of the photos have been real? What about the unidentified **sonar** 'hits'? If they weren't shoals of fish, what were they? And what sort of creature could the monster be – a relic from **prehistoric** times or a modern mammal or fish?

Try to keep an open mind. Remember that if scientists throughout history had not bothered to investigate everything that appeared at first to be strange or mysterious, many scientific discoveries would never have been made at all.

Glossary

animate something which is alive

cryptozoology the study of prehistoric or ancient animals, thought to be extinct

extinct a plant or animal which has died out for ever

filter-feeder an animal, such as a whale or a large shark, which feeds on tiny plants and animals which it sieves from the water

flotilla a small fleet of boats or ships

geology the scientific study of the rocks of the Earth's crust

GPS (Global Positioning System) a very accurate way of finding your position on land, sea or in the air. Information is sent from satellites orbiting the Earth to a small computer on the ground. From the satellite signals, the computer works out your location.

hallucination when you think you see or hear something which is not really there

hibernate to go into a deep sleep or period of inactivity. Some animals hibernate during the cold winter months to save energy when food is scarce.

Ice Age a time when snow and ice covered much of the Earth. The last Ice Age finished about 12,000 years ago.

marine biologist a scientist who studies life in the sea

migration a long journey made by some fish, birds and mammals between their feeding and breeding grounds

NASA (National Aeronautics and Space Administration) the organization in the USA that controls the US space programme

naturalist a scientist who studies the natural world

nutrients substances in the water which provide food and nourishment for living things

optical illusion a picture which tricks the eye into thinking it shows something which it does not show

phenomenon a remarkable or unexplained happening

plankton tiny plants and animals which drift on the surface of water and provide food for many other animals

plesiosaur a long-necked prehistoric reptile

predator any animal that lives by feeding on other animals

prehistoric before recorded time

rhomboid diamond-shaped

sediment the layer of mud, sand and rock which lies on the bottom of a lake or river

sonar short for 'sound navigation ranging'. Sonar instruments use sound to map a lake or sea-floor. Beeps of sound bounce off objects or underwater features and send back echoes. These are picked up by an on-ship computer and used to draw up a map.

superimposed placed on top of something else, such as something which is added to a photograph

wake the track left on the surface of the water by a moving ship or boat

zoologist a scientist who studies animals

Index